# MANAGEMENT
# WASTE

## STUDY GUIDE

**5**

STEPS TO
CLEAN UP THE MESS
AND LEAD WITH PURPOSE

## LARRY O'DONNELL III

*Former President of Waste Management and Featured
on the Premiere Episode of the Hit Television Series*
**UNDERCOVER BOSS**

Servant Ministries Foundation
AUSTIN, TEXAS

ISBN: 979-8-218-21407-4 (Print)

Some of the anecdotal illustrations used in this book are true to life and are included with the permission of the persons mentioned. All other illustrations are composites of real situations, and any resemblance to people living or dead is purely coincidental. For permission to reuse any content, contact Larry O'Donnell at larry@larryodonnell.com.

All Scripture quotations, unless otherwise indicated, are taken from the Holy Bible, New International Version®, NIV® Copyright © 1973, 1978, 1984, 2011 by Biblica, Inc.® Used by permission.

Scripture quotations marked ESV are taken from The Holy Bible, English Standard Version. ESV® Text Edition: 2016. Copyright © 2001 by Crossway Bibles, a publishing ministry of Good News Publishers. Used by permission.

Scripture quotations marked NASB are taken from the New American Standard Bible Copyright © 1960, 1962, 1963, 1968, 1971, 1972, 1973, 1975, 1977, 1995 by The Lockman Foundation. Used by permission.

Please note that pronouns that are references to God, God the Father, Jesus, and the Holy Spirit are always capitalized from the quoted Scripture to aid in the understanding of the lesson.

Library of Congress Control Number: 2023910607

Printed in the United States of America

27 26 25 24 23     1 2 3 4 5

# MANAGEMENT
# WASTE

**STUDY GUIDE**

## DEDICATION

*This book is dedicated to
my son Larry O'Donnell IV, his wife Christina,
and my brand new first grandson Lawrence Reeves O'Donnell
(and all my future grandchildren).*

What gifts God has given us in our children and grandchildren, true miracles and blessings indeed! I hope and pray that my awesome grandson and all my future grandchildren and descendants in the years to come will grow up to love Jesus as much as I do! I hope and pray they have the burning desire to read the Bible and grow in their personal relationship with their Lord and Savior Jesus Christ! May *Management Waste: 5 Steps to Clean Up the Mess and Lead with Purpose* and this Study Guide be of help to them and others who seek to be a servant of the Most High God. Thank You, Jesus, for giving me the will and the way to be Your instrument to write *Management Waste* and this Study Guide to help others grow in their personal relationship with You and become servant leaders as Jesus modeled. And most of all, thank You for Your grace and love, and for providing me Your free gift of my faith and salvation, and a pathway for the forgiveness of my sin and eternal life with You!

# Contents

Acknowledgments ................................................................... ix

Introduction to the Study Guide ............................................ 1

1. Why Management Waste? ................................................ 5
   *Introduction*

2. Convertible Leadership ..................................................... 11
   *Top Down vs. Bottom-Up*

3. Wasted Management .......................................................... 19
   *Commitment*

4. Trash Talking ..................................................................... 27
   *Listening*

5. Game Changer .................................................................... 35
   *Empathy*

6. The Loneliest Job in the World ......................................... 43
   *Accountability*

7. "Dumbster" ......................................................................... 51
   *Notice*

8. Recycling: One Man's Trash
   Is Another Man's Treasure ................................................. 61
   *Joy and Contentment Are Infectious*

9. Taking Out the Trash ........................................................ 67
   *What Do You Need to Turn Over to God?*

10. Exit Strategy ......................................................... 73
   *When You Leave Your Job*

11. The Ultimate Undercover Boss ........................................ 81
   *Concluding Remarks*

Closing Thoughts .................................................... 99

Larry O'Donnell III Short Bio ............................................. 101

# Acknowledgments

Shortly after the publishing of my first book, *Management Waste: 5 Steps to Clean Up the Mess and Lead with Purpose,* I began getting requests to write a Study Guide for people to use in their individual and small group study of the book and the Scripture referenced in the book. After much prayer, research, and drafting, as well as feedback and input from readers, this Study Guide has now become a reality.

I want to thank Teresa Rossy, who has helped me immensely during the drafting of this Study Guide through several iterations. Her time, dedication, and work on this Study Guide, as well as her encouragement to me, helped bring together what I hope will be an excellent companion to the book, as people seek a deeper understanding of what Jesus taught us in His Word and by the way He modeled Servant Leadership for us.

I also want to thank the members of my weekly Bible Study for their constant encouragement to me at our Bible Study each week, as I tested many of the concepts that are contained in this Study Guide on them. I am grateful for their friendship and fellowship. They are a highlight of my week each week as we join together to study God's Word, and make our study available to others through our recorded podcast each week (available for you to subscribe for free on my website: www.larryodonnell .com).

I also thank my loving and dedicated wife, Dare. She is my source of continued love, grace, patience, and support, and models to me what unconditional love really means each and every day. She is the best gift that God has given to me outside of the gift of His Son Jesus, my faith, and my salvation. God knew what He was doing when He gave Dare to me, and I can't imagine life on this side without her.

And finally, I thank my "best daughter" Linley, for being God's instrument to bring about a tremendous change in my life. What an amazing gift from God you are to me!

I hope and pray that this Study Guide will serve as a useful vehicle for people to grow in their understanding of what it means to be a Servant Leader, while at the same time helping them grow in their personal relationship with Jesus as their Lord and Savior. In that way, we can each avoid becoming Management Waste—wasting the gifts, talents, relationships, and opportunities, that God has given us—so that we can each hear "Well done, good and faithful servant!" when we join Jesus in Heaven!

May God continue to bless each of you!

Larry O'Donnell III
June 2023

# Introduction
# to the Study Guide

*"I have written this book to help Christian leaders*
*see how God wants us to be Servant Leaders."*
— Larry O'Donnell

*Management Waste* is an inspirational and practical tool to help readers grow in their relationship with God. Larry O'Donnell shares challenges and tragedies from his life hoping that others will not have to experience a catastrophic life event for God to get their attention and that instead, the Word of God and practical leadership advice will shape and form them into the Servant Leaders that our world needs.

This Study Guide is intended to be used by small groups of people who share a common desire to grow as Christian leaders. Because Larry shares freely from his own life experiences—both the highs and lows—it is my hope that the members of your group will covenant together to be transparent with one another in a trusting relationship to help make this study group more effective. You might consider beginning your group with a covenant agreement. Here are some ideas to get you started:

1. We agree that what is shared in the group will remain confidential and no one will repeat what is said in our sessions outside the group without permission.

2. We recognize that we all have areas in our life that can be improved and brought into more alignment with God's will

for our life. With confidentiality in place, we will each commit to be as transparent with the group as we comfortably can, knowing that the more we each open up to one another about our struggles and challenges, the closer we will become as a group, and the more impactful and meaningful our discussions will be.

3. Our group will seek God's guidance in prayer each time we meet, and we will pray for one another between meeting times.

4. We will respect the life experiences, Bible interpretations, personalities, and theological perspectives of each member— looking for Biblically-based common ground rather than focusing on what separates us.

5. We will agree upon a meeting structure and cadence that works for all, respecting time, space, and leadership considerations. We will then commit and be accountable to the group to be present for, and engaged during, our agreed sessions.

6. We agree that each session will have a leader to lead the group discussion, help keep the discussions on track, and help insure that each attendee has an opportunity to speak if so desired. Your group may choose for one person to lead all the sessions, or assign shared/alternating leadership roles/times.

7. We will come to each meeting prepared, having read the Chapter that will be discussed in advance of the meeting, as well as spending time on the applicable Chapter in this Study Guide.

8. We will each commit to not dominate the conversation, will respect the leader's efforts to lead the discussion, and give space for each attendee to participate in the discussions. We will come together with high expectations of what God will

shape and form in us as a result of our commitment to this group.

This Study Guide is designed for the meeting sessions to flow in this way:

**Making Connections**—What story from Larry's life resonated with you? What story from your own life came to mind when you read this Chapter?

**Management Waste**—Is there a current situation that you are focused on as a result of this Chapter? How might our time together strengthen you so that you avoid beginning or continuing in a *Management Waste* trajectory (wasting the life, opportunities, gifts, and relationships that God has given to you)? Each person will be asked to share this with the group as he or she is comfortable. It is important for all to understand that the group time is not to be used for solving these problems, but rather for offering them up for God's care. (See Galatians 6:2-6)

**Scripture Study**—Each session will include at least one or two passages from Scripture for the group to read together and dialogue about. Take time to allow each person who wishes to share their own reflection on the passage to do so. Remember that some will be more comfortable with Scripture engagement than others. Guiding questions are provided for the leader. Note that all Scripture references are to the New International Version (NIV) unless otherwise indicated (used with permission), however, pronouns that are references to God, God the Father, Jesus, and the Holy Spirit are always capitalized to aid in the understanding of the lesson. References to the New American Standard (NASB) and the English Standard Version (ESV) are also used with permission.

**Servant Leadership**—Share with your group one small step you will take this week to grow as a *Servant Leader*—to be more like Jesus.

**Pray**—Always close your time together in prayer. This is a wonderful time to be creative with a variety of ways to pray, such as (1) having one person open and close the prayer, with others speaking up with their own prayers in between; or (2) breaking into pairs to pray in groups of two; or (3) anything else you may decide. Do your best to avoid having a "designated prayer leader." Servant leaders commit to praying for others, and your group gatherings are an excellent place to practice. We will provide you some prayer suggestions at the end of each Chapter.

## CHAPTER 1

# Why Management Waste?

## Introduction

### *Making Connections*

Larry told two stories from his life in this Chapter that represented a challenge and a tragedy, or shipwreck. The business challenge to turn around Waste Management was a learning experience that stretched him professionally and developed his leadership style and practices.

The story of Linley's life-changing medical challenge tragedy as an infant stretched Larry's faith and relationship with God.

### *Reflection Questions*

- What story from Larry's life resonated with you?




- What story from your own life came to mind when you read this Chapter?

- What has been your biggest professional challenge so far? What is your biggest takeaway from that period in your life?

_____

_____

_____

- What has been your biggest personal challenge so far? How has that affected your relationship with God?

_____

_____

_____

## Management Waste

If you are willing, share with the group a current situation you are facing as a leader that relates to this Chapter. Consider how the time with your group and in Bible study might strengthen you so that you avoid *Management Waste* in this situation. Remember, this time is not meant for the group to attempt to solve this problem, but rather, you are offering situations up for God's help and direction (**Galatians 6:2-6**).

## Scripture Study

**John 9:1-7**

> *As He went along, He saw a man blind from birth. ² His disciples asked Him, "Rabbi, who sinned, this man or his parents, that he was born blind?"*
>
> *³ "Neither this man nor his parents sinned," said Jesus, "but this happened so that the works of God might be displayed in him. ⁴ As long as it is day, we must do the works of Him who sent Me. Night is coming, when*

*no one can work.* ⁵ *While I am in the world, I am the light of the world."*

⁶ *After saying this, He spit on the ground, made some mud with the saliva, and put it on the man's eyes.*

⁷ *"Go," He told him, "wash in the Pool of Siloam" (this word means "Sent"). So the man went and washed, and came home seeing.*

1. What does Jesus say about the connection between sin and suffering?

 

 

 

2. Consider **John 9:1-7** as the first scene in a play. Continue reading John 9 together and make note of the reactions of the neighbors, the Pharisees, the man's parents, and Jesus Himself.

 

 

 

3. Next, notice the blind man's actions and words. What marks of discipleship do you see in him?

 

 

 

4. What do the Pharisees and their followers (religious leaders of the Jews in Jesus' day) do and say in this passage? What does Jesus say to them in verses 38-41? What dangers do you see as a result of spiritual blindness in this story? What are the spiritual blessings of "seeing" Jesus by faith?

 

5. Jesus is all over the place in this Chapter! Spend time with your group noticing all that He says and does in **John 9**. How has Jesus sought you as He did the blind man? How are you continuing to encounter Jesus and worship Him more fully?

6. What works of God does Jesus want to display in your life to others? What do you think God's intended purpose is for you as a follower of Jesus? What do you think He wants to accomplish in and through you? Are you resisting His direction? If so, what is holding you back?

## 2 Timothy 3:16

*All Scripture is God-breathed and is useful for teaching, rebuking, correcting and training in righteousness.*

1. What do each of the "functions" of Scripture named in this verse mean to you? Read the verse in several translations for ideas.

2. The Biblical principle that Paul is teaching in **2 Timothy 3:16** is at work in the story of the man born blind. Jesus corrects, rebukes, teaches, and trains the disciples as He speaks to their mistaken belief that the blind man's affliction is caused by his (or his parents') sin. Can you think of a time when God's Word worked in your own life in one of these four ways?

_____

_____

_____

3. What are areas in your own life that need correcting and that are preventing you from becoming more Christ-like, fully able to serve as Christ's ambassador and representative to others?

_____

_____

_____

## Servant Leadership

Share with your group one small step you will take this week to grow as a *Servant Leader*—to be more like Jesus.

## Pray

Please close your session in prayer in whatever manner your group chooses. You can select one person to open and close the prayer, with others speaking up with their own prayers in between, or break into pairs to pray in groups of two, or anything else you may decide. Remember, it doesn't matter what you have been in the past. Some suggestions to include in your prayer from this Chapter:

- Lord, I am willing to be made willing to become more of Servant Leader. Help me see where I need to make changes in my life so that I will place others ahead of myself. Help me rely less on myself and more on You.
- Make me into the leader, colleague, friend, spouse, and parent that you want me to be.
- Help me reflect You and represent You to those I encounter in the coming week.
- Show me a specific area you desire to transform in my life, with the power of the Holy Spirit working in me.
- We pray this in Jesus' Name. Amen!

## *Additional Notes*

## CHAPTER 2

# Convertible Leadership
## Top Down vs. Bottom-Up

### *Making Connections*

Larry shared his experiences working for "top-down" leaders who functioned from a "convertible leadership" model. He said that top-down leaders expect everyone to serve the leader, and the leader directs others to perform in a way that serves the interests of the leader. A top-down leader wants everyone focused on them as the leader, like they are riding around in a convertible with the top down for all to admire while the leader is self-absorbed (and self-deceived about their leadership ability).

### *Reflection Questions*

- Do you have a top-down leadership story to share—either from your own role as a top-down leader or from working in this type of environment?

- What did you learn from that experience?

---

---

- Conversely, have you experienced learning from a Servant Leader—someone who cared about you personally and was motivated by helping you?

---

---

---

- What did you learn from that experience?

---

---

---

## *Management Waste*

If you are willing, share with the group a current challenging situation you are facing as a leader. Consider how the time with your group and in Bible study might strengthen you so that you avoid practicing or being consumed by *convertible leadership* in this situation and becoming *Management Waste*.

## *Scripture Study*

**Matthew 20:20-28**

> *Then the mother of Zebedee's sons came to Jesus with her sons and, kneeling down, asked a favor of Him. [21] "What is it you want?" He asked. She said, "Grant that one of these two sons of mine may sit at Your right and the other at Your left in Your kingdom."*

> [22] *"You don't know what you are asking," Jesus said to them. "Can you drink the cup I am going to drink?"*
> *"We can," they answered.*
> [23] *Jesus said to them, "You will indeed drink from My cup, but to sit at My right or left is not for Me to grant. These places belong to those for whom they have been prepared by My Father."*
> [24] *When the ten heard about this, they were indignant with the two brothers.* [25] *Jesus called them together and said, "You know that the rulers of the Gentiles lord it over them, and their high officials exercise authority over them.* [26] *Not so with you. Instead, whoever wants to become great among you must be your servant,* [27] *and whoever wants to be first must be your slave—* [28] *just as the Son of Man did not come to be served, but to serve, and to give His life as a ransom for many."*

In this passage, Jesus makes His third and final "passion prediction" in which He specifically tells His disciples that He is going to be crucified in Jerusalem.

1. Read the first passion prediction in **Matthew 16:21-28**. What does Jesus say His followers must do in this passage?

_____

_____

_____

2. Read the second passion prediction in **Matthew 17:22-23** and **Mark 9:30-37**. What does Jesus say a person who wants to be first must do?

_____

_____

_____

3. Read the third passion prediction in **Matthew 20:17-28** and **Mark 10:32-45**. What does Jesus say a person who wants to be great must be and do?

_____

_____

_____

4. In all of these passages, what is the disciples' reaction? How are they described?

_____

_____

_____

5. In light of what Jesus was teaching His disciples at the time James and John asked for special positions of authority, what stands out to you about their question and the reaction of the other disciples?

_____

_____

_____

6. What do you think Jesus means by "drink the cup that I drink, or be baptized with the baptism that I am baptized with?"

_____

_____

_____

## *Servant Leadership*

**John 13:1-5; 12-17**

In **John 13:1-5, 12-17**, Jesus models Servant Leadership to the disciples by washing their feet, which was one of the lowliest jobs during that time:

> *It was just before the Passover Festival. Jesus knew that the hour had come for Him to leave this world and go to the Father. Having loved His own who were in the world, He loved them to the end. [2] The evening meal was in progress, and the devil had already prompted Judas, the son of Simon Iscariot, to betray Jesus. [3] Jesus knew that the Father had put all things under His power, and that He had come from God and was returning to God; [4] so He got up from the meal, took off His outer clothing, and wrapped a towel around His waist. [5] After that, He poured water into a basin and began to wash His disciples' feet, drying them with the towel that was wrapped around Him . . . [12] When He had finished washing their feet, He put on His clothes and returned to His place. "Do you understand what I have done for you?" [13] He asked them. "You call me 'Teacher' and 'Lord,' and rightly so, for that is what I am. [14] Now that I, your Lord and Teacher, have washed your feet, you also should wash one another's feet. [15] I have set you an example that you should do as I have done for you. [16] Very truly I tell you, no servant is greater than his master, nor is a messenger greater than the one who sent him. [17] Now that you know these things, you will be blessed if you do them.*

Try applying Jesus' example of Servant Leadership to your own life—especially in your role as a leader:

1. Write a statement that expresses what Jesus wants us to do as Servant Leaders based on your Bible study this week.

_____

_____

_____

2. Record a time when you functioned as a "top-down" leader. In hindsight, was your action based on ignorance or deliberate disobedience (focusing on yourself rather than others)?

_____

_____

_____

3. Make notes about a time when you demonstrated Christ's example of Servant Leadership, even though obedience required sacrifice on your part.

_____

_____

_____

4. Pay attention to the opportunities you have this week to practice Servant Leadership — serving others with the Lord as your leader. Notice your attitude toward Jesus, your tendency to ignore His call to place others ahead of yourself and serve them, and your willingness to follow Jesus and the example He gave us.

_____

_____

_____

5. Share with your group one small step you will take this week to grow as a *Servant Leader*—to be more like Jesus.

---

---

---

## *Pray*

Please close your session in prayer in whatever manner your group chooses. You can select one person to open and close the prayer, with others speaking up with their own prayers in between, or break into pairs to pray in groups of two, or anything else you may decide. Remember, it doesn't matter what you have been in the past, what are you going to ask the Holy Spirit to help you change beginning today? Following are suggestions to include in your prayer from this Chapter:

- Jesus, You are my Lord and Savior, the promised Messiah. Thank you for living your life as a perfect example of Servant Leadership. Help me to see You clearly and trust in You when I am called to serve others, rather than trusting in myself and my own plans.

- Lord, our human tendency to grab for power and control is not the way You modeled or lived and gave Your life for us. Help us live with a focus on serving others, and placing their interests ahead of our own.

- Lord, show us this week when we are drifting toward top-down leadership and away from Servant Leadership. Fill us with empathy, humility, and love for others. We are willing to be made willing to serve others. Help us begin to serve others as You modeled for us.

- We pray this in Jesus' Name. Amen!

## Additional Notes

# Wasted Management

## Commitment

### Making Connections

In Chapter 3, Larry discusses the first characteristic of Servant Leadership: *Commitment*. Larry relates stories from his career experience to illustrate several key practices that show commitment to the success of others. Be sure to reread the Forward by Jim Fish, CEO of Waste Management along with Chapter 3. Doing so will give you both perspectives—the Servant Leader's and the person being influenced.

### Reflection Questions

- In this section of *Management Waste*, Larry introduces an acronym to help remember five key characteristics of Servant Leadership. **CLEAN** stands for *Commitment, Listening, Empathy, Accountability*, and *Notice*. The first characteristic is commitment. What does commitment mean to you? How do you show your commitment to the well-being of others at work or at home?

- Can you share a story from your life about the effect of knowing that another person has been committed to your success as a whole person?

  _____

  _____

  _____

- In this Chapter, Larry shares one of his favorite stories about empowerment of others in his story about "Project Yellow Tail." Do you have a story where you have seen the success of giving up control and empowering others? Is there an opportunity that has come to your mind where you can empower others beginning today?

  _____

  _____

  _____

## *Management Waste*

Is there a current situation that you are focused on as a result of reading the many management strategies and suggestions in this Chapter? Will you share with the group a need you are hoping to address through increased commitment to either learning from a leader or being a leader who is committed to and pouring into others?

  _____

  _____

  _____

## *Scripture Study*

**Luke 9:1-2**

> *When Jesus had called the Twelve together, He gave them power and authority to drive out all demons and to cure diseases, and He sent them out to proclaim the kingdom of God and to heal the sick.*

Beginning in **Luke 4**, after Jesus' 40 days in the wilderness, He returns to Galilee, filled with the power of the Spirit. There, in His home synagogue in Nazareth, He read from the scroll of Isaiah (**Isaiah 61:1-2**), announcing His ministry mission with these words:

> *The Spirit of the Lord is upon me, because He has anointed Me to bring Good News to the poor. He has sent Me to proclaim release to the captives and recovery of sight to the blind, to let the oppressed go free, to proclaim the year of the Lord's favor.*

(Note that it is interesting that Jesus stopped short before finishing the entire verse of **Isaiah 61:2**. Most likely that was because **Isaiah 61:1** through the first part of verse 2 are prophesying Jesus' First Coming (and Jesus is now reading aloud those verses about Himself and His First Coming right then in their presence), and the second part of **Isaiah 61:2** that Jesus didn't read aloud at that time was prophecy about Jesus' Second Coming in judgment which would be later.)

1. From that point in Luke's gospel until Chapter 9, Jesus does just that—teaching, healing, calling His disciples and teaching them the meaning of the Hebrew Scriptures and how to pray. Now, He is ready—as their Servant Leader—to send them out to do what He has been modeling.

List all the things Jesus does for His disciples in these two verses.

What does He empower them to do?

What charge does He give them?

_____

_____

_____

2. How do you think they responded to Jesus' instructions and expectations?

_____

_____

_____

3. Jesus' charge required the Twelve to rely on Him and embark on a God-sized task. The Christian's charge is the same today. How are you responding to the call to discipleship in your own life? (Read and discuss **2 Timothy 2:2 (NASB)**:

> *The things which you have heard from me in the presence of many witnesses, entrust these to faithful people who will be able to teach others also.*

In what ways are you relying on your own power?

Where do you need to humbly ask the Holy Spirit to empower your leadership, discipleship, and mission?

Who could you pour into to disciple and help them mature in their faith to become disciple makers?

_____

_____

_____

## *Servant Leadership*

**Matthew 25:14-28**

*Again, it will be like a man going on a journey, who called his servants and entrusted his wealth to them. [15] To one he gave five bags of gold, to another two bags, and to another one bag, each according to his ability. Then he went on his journey. [16] The man who had received five bags of gold went at once and put his money to work and gained five bags more. [17] So also, the one with two bags of gold gained two more. [18] But the man who had received one bag went off, dug a hole in the ground and hid his master's money.*

*[19] After a long time the master of those servants returned and settled accounts with them. [20] The man who had received five bags of gold brought the other five. 'Master,' he said, 'you entrusted me with five bags of gold. See, I have gained five more.'*

*[21] His master replied, 'Well done, good and faithful servant! You have been faithful with a few things; I will put you in charge of many things. Come and share your master's happiness!'*

*[22] The man with two bags of gold also came. 'Master,' he said, 'you entrusted me with two bags of gold; see, I have gained two more.'*

*[23] His master replied, 'Well done, good and faithful servant! You have been faithful with a few things; I will put you in charge of many things. Come and share your master's happiness!'*

*[24] Then the man who had received one bag of gold came. 'Master,' he said, 'I knew that you are a hard man, harvesting where you have not sown and gathering where you have not scattered seed. [25] So I was afraid*

*and went out and hid your gold in the ground. See, here is what belongs to you.'*

*[26] His master replied, 'You wicked, lazy servant! So you knew that I harvest where I have not sown and gather where I have not scattered seed? [27] Well then, you should have put my money on deposit with the bankers, so that when I returned I would have received it back with interest.*

*[28] 'So take the bag of gold from him and give it to the one who has ten bags.'*

Near the end of his ministry, Jesus taught this parable about faithfulness and commitment. (A similar but different parable is found in **Luke 19:11-27**). Larry writes, "This parable illustrates that we are to be committed to doing our best with whatever God has given to us . . . then, when we demonstrate we are capable with the smaller things, we will be given larger areas of responsibility. I have found the most effective leaders have been followers first."

1. Give an example of "follow-ship" in your own work or home life. What did you learn from that? How might you use some examples from your own life as you mentor younger leaders looking to move into positions of increased responsibility?

_____

_____

_____

2. Jesus taught this parable just days before His disciples (the same ones who had been sent to proclaim the Kingdom, cure diseases, heal, and cast out demons in His name) would be faced with seeing Him arrested, beaten, and crucified. Their faith would be tested mightily. Why do you

think Jesus taught them about faithfulness in small things at a time like that?

_____

_____

_____

3. Is there something you are currently "entrusted with" by God to steward? Describe your commitment to manage this faithfully. What help do you need from God or others to accomplish this task?

_____

_____

_____

4. Share with your group one small step you will take this week to grow as a *Servant Leader*—to be more like Jesus.

_____

_____

_____

## *Pray*

Please close your session in prayer in whatever manner your group chooses. You can select one person to open and close the prayer, with others speaking up with their own prayers in between, or break into pairs to pray in groups of two, or anything else you may decide. Remember, it doesn't matter what you have been in the past, what are you going to ask the Holy Spirit to help you change beginning today? Following are suggestions to include in your prayer from this Chapter:

• God, show us how to be more committed followers of Christ.

- Lord, I am thankful for the people who have been leaders and supporters in my life. Show me ways to express my thanks to them.

- God, we ask for increased humility—so that we can continue to learn from You and from those You have placed in our lives. Help us be coachable, teachable, and willing to grow as leaders.

- Lord, please guide me to the people You want me to lead and help them mature and become disciple makers. Fill me with the Holy Spirit, so that the guidance I give will come from You.

- We pray this in Jesus' Name. Amen!

## Additional Notes

_____

_____

_____

_____

_____

_____

_____

_____

_____

_____

_____

_____

_____

# Trash Talking
## Listening

### *Making Connections*

In Chapter 4, Larry discusses the second characteristic of Servant Leadership: *Listening*. Larry relates stories from his career to illustrate the value he has found in listening to others and acting on what he learns. He practiced listening and he led his management team to do the same. Larry says, "Another thing happened from doing that (listening). It got around the company. People began to trust us. The employees saw we not only valued their opinions, but we implemented many of them . . . It became all about *us*, not about the leaders. It was powerful indeed!" (p. 58-59, *Management Waste*)

### *Reflection Questions:*

- In this section of *Management Waste*, Larry focuses on listening—one of the five key characteristics of Servant Leadership. When you think about listening, what comes to mind first—yourself as a listener or your need to be heard?

MANAGEMENT WASTE STUDY GUIDE

- Can you share a story from your life about a time when someone demonstrated that they cared for you by the way they listened to you and truly heard you?

_____

_____

_____

## *Management Waste*

Is there a current situation that you are focused on as a result of reading the management stories, strategies and suggestions in this Chapter? Will you share with the group a need you are hoping to address through becoming a better listener?

_____

_____

_____

## *Scripture Study*

Scripture is full of wise counsel and good examples that speak to the value of listening. Read these passages from the Old and New Testaments and share in your group your impressions of each example.

> **Proverbs 1:5:** *Let the wise listen and add to their learning, and let the discerning get guidance.*

> **Proverbs 12:15:** *The way of fools seems right to them, but the wise listen to advice.*

> **Proverbs 19:20:** *Listen to advice and accept instruction, that you may gain wisdom in the future. (ESV)*

**1 Samuel 3:8-11:** *A third time the Lord called, "Samuel!" And Samuel got up and went to Eli and said, "Here I am; you called me." Then Eli realized that the Lord was calling the boy. So Eli told Samuel, "Go and lie down, and if He calls you, say, 'Speak Lord, for your servant is listening.'" So Samuel went and lay down in his place. The Lord came and stood there, calling as at the other times, "Samuel! Samuel!" Then Samuel said, "Speak, for Your servant is listening." And the Lord said to Samuel: "See, I am about to do something in Israel that will make the ears of everyone who hears about it tingle."*

**Luke 2:46-47:** *After three days they found Him (Jesus) sitting in the temple courts, listening to them and asking them questions. Everyone who heard Him was amazed at His understanding and His answers.*

**Luke 3:21-22:** *When all the people were being baptized, Jesus was baptized too. And as He was praying, Heaven was opened and the Holy Spirit descended on Him in bodily form like a dove. And a voice came from Heaven: "You are my Son, whom I love; with You I am well pleased."*

**Luke 6:12-13:** *One of those days Jesus went out to a mountainside to pray, and spent the night praying to God. When morning came, He called His disciples to Him and chose twelve of them, whom He also designated apostles.*

**Luke 9:35-36:** *A voice came from the cloud, saying, "This is my Son, whom I have chosen; listen to Him." When the voice had spoken, they found that Jesus was* *alone. The disciples kept this to themselves and did not tell anyone at that time what they had seen.*

**Luke 10:38-39:** *As Jesus and His disciples were on their way, He came to a village where a woman named Martha opened her home to Him. She had a sister called Mary, who sat at the Lord's feet listening to what He said.*

**John 16:12-13:** *"I have much more to say to you, more than you can now bear. But when He, the Spirit of truth, comes, He will guide you into all the truth. He will not speak on His own; He will speak only what He hears, and He will tell you what is yet to come."*

## *Servant Leadership*

### Listening and Doing: James 1:19-25

[19] *My dear brothers and sisters, take note of this: Everyone should be quick to listen, slow to speak and slow to become angry,* [20] *because human anger does not produce the righteousness that God desires.* [21] *Therefore, get rid of all moral filth and the evil that is so prevalent and humbly accept the Word planted in you, which can save you.*

[22] *Do not merely listen to the Word, and so deceive yourselves. Do what it says.* [23] *Anyone who listens to the Word but does not do what it says is like someone who looks at his face in a mirror* [24] *and, after looking at himself, goes away and immediately forgets what he looks like.* [25] *But whoever looks intently into the perfect law that gives freedom, and continues in it—not forgetting what they have heard, but doing it—they will be blessed in what they do.*

1. James is describing a process that leads to God's righteousness being developed in the lives of disciples. What steps are outlined in verse 19? Why is it important to control our anger and our tongues?

2. What next steps in this process does James lay out in verses 21-22? What does it mean to you to "humbly accept the word planted in you?" How has receiving and acting on the Word of God led to and supported your salvation?

3. In Chapter 4 of *Management Waste*, Larry shared many examples of the actions he took in his company based on what he learned from listening to his co-workers. James says that "whoever looks intently into the perfect law that gives freedom, and **continues in it** . . . will be blessed in what they do." Other versions of the Bible translate continues in it as "perseverance" and "don't forget what you heard." What connections do you see between Larry's leadership examples and the Biblical advice in this passage?

4. What are some next steps that you can take with your team, friends, family, or spouse, to show them that you are listening and that you truly care and are interested in them? How can

you make them feel that you place them ahead of your own interests?

_____

_____

_____

5. Watch this video: https://www.youtube.com/watch?v=-4ED-hdAHrOg (*It's Not About The Nail*) and discuss your reactions. Do you see yourself in this video? How so?

_____

_____

_____

## *Pray*

Please close your session in prayer in whatever manner your group chooses. You can select one person to open and close the prayer, with others speaking up with their own prayers in between, or break into pairs to pray in groups of two, or anything else you may decide. Remember, it doesn't matter what you have been in the past, what are you going to ask the Holy Spirit to help you change beginning today? Following are suggestions to include in your prayer from this Chapter:

- God, give me ears to hear what You are saying to me.

- God, forgive me for talking more than I listen to You and to others.

- Lord, thank You for the people I am surrounded by at work. Help me listen more intently to them.

- Thank You, Holy Spirit for guiding me into all the truth.

- Lord, give me humility and courage to act on what I hear from You and from the people You have placed in my life.
- God, I ask You to open up the opportunity for me to have a meaningful conversation with a co-worker, friend, or family member this week.
- We pray this in Jesus' Name. Amen!

## Additional Notes

# CHAPTER 5

# Game Changer
## Empathy

## *Making Connections*

In Chapter 5, Larry discusses the third characteristic of Servant Leadership: *Empathy*. Larry shares how God transformed him into a person with greater empathy through the tragedy he went through with his daughter. He learned that "we can follow Jesus' command to us to love others as ourselves by demonstrating empathy to others—caring and having concern about others in a way you can sense their feelings to such an extent you share in their suffering." We must develop self-awareness and put empathy into action to unlock our kindness and compassion. Then, others will know that we truly care and that we have the love of Jesus living within us.

## *Reflection Questions:*

- In what area of your life could deeper empathy be a game changer for you?

---

---

---

- What cultural roadblocks exist in your organization that could be eliminated with an increased corporate or community focus on empathy as a higher value?

  _____

  _____

  _____

- How could increased empathy improve your relationships with your spouse, family, friends, and colleagues?

  _____

  _____

  _____

## Management Waste

Is there a personal situation that has the potential to be improved if you were able to be more empathetic? Will you share with the group how you imagine God wants to use you as a Servant Leader in these situations?

_____

_____

_____

## Scripture Study

Jesus commonly asked questions as a method of spiritual teaching. Jesus did not ask "gotcha" questions that set up the question's receivers to be rebuked or chastised. Rather, Jesus asked questions in order to aid the growth of those to whom the questions were intended. He probed the faith, understanding, and experience of persons around Him in order to help them know themselves better . . . to see the limitations of their present faith . . . and their need to move onward in their depth of communion with Him and with the Father.

**Questions God Asks in Scripture**

Read each passage below. Be prepared during your group time to meet in pairs, with each pair taking one of the stories and sharing their answers.

1. *"Where are you?"* Read **Genesis 1-3**. In Genesis 3, God asks Adam this question when he and Eve were hiding from Him after eating the forbidden fruit. God always pursues us in love. God is longing for our companionship and will search for us until He finds us. How did God show compassion for Adam and Eve (see **Genesis 3:21**)? How can we make God's love and compassion real for others?

_____

_____

_____

2. *"What is that in your hand?"* The question comes from the story of Moses. Read **Exodus 3:1-14, and 4:1-5**. Moses had a list of excuses for why he could not say yes to God. God's question was aimed at showing Moses that he already had everything he needed to fulfill God's calling. Read **Exodus 4:11-17** and **2 Peter 1:3**. In many respects, we are like Moses, filled with both excuses and something to offer God. We have three key items in our hands: our abilities, life experiences, and inadequacies. List some of yours.

_____

_____

_____

3. *"What are you looking for?"* **Read John 1:35-42.** This is the first question Jesus asks in the Gospels. John the Baptizer was walking with two of his disciples. Jesus walked by and John called out "Look, there is the Lamb of God" and the two disciples began to follow Jesus. Jesus saw them following Him and asked, "What are you looking for?" or "What do you want?" What do you think Jesus meant by this question? How would you have reacted had you been with the disciples and Jesus asked you this question? Jesus asked the first disciples then and asks us now to listen to our hearts; to discover what we desire most; and to ask Him for what we want. What are your heart's desires? How do you communicate these with the Lord? Is what you are looking for aligned with what God has planned for you? Do you tell God what is on your mind, but then say "But Your will be done!" Read **Matthew 26:36-46.**

---

---

---

4. *"Who do you say that I am?"* Read **Matthew 16:13-20** and **Mark 8:27-30.** Jesus' disciples had been following Him for an extended period of time when He asked them this question. The crowds who heard Him teach and those who were bent on destroying Him were also intensely questioning who this teacher and healer was. It was time to measure the faith of His disciples. They had knowledge of Jesus and faith in Him. We too can know Jesus through historical (Bible) knowledge and personal experience. List seven answers to the question "Who do you say that I am?" Notice which aspect of your understanding of Christ needs more attention: Biblical or personal.

---

---

Other questions for further study:

- *"Why are you angry?"* Genesis 4
- *"Why are you crying?"* John 20
- *"Do you want to get well?"* John 5
- *"What is it you want Me to do for you?"* Mark 10

## *Servant Leadership*

**Philippians 2:3-8**

> *Do nothing out of selfish ambition or vain conceit. Rather, in humility value others above yourselves, ⁴ not looking to your own interests but each of you to the interests of the others.*
>
> *⁵ In your relationships with one another, have the same mindset as Christ Jesus: ⁶ Who, being in very nature God, did not consider equality with God some-thing to be used to His own advantage; ⁷ rather, He made Himself nothing by taking the very nature of a servant, being made in human likeness. ⁸ And being found in appearance as a man, He humbled Himself by becoming obedient to death—even death on a cross!*

Jesus was the ultimate game changer. He came to earth in human form, transforming Himself in order to transform the world and transform us. His act of obedience to God the Father led Him down a path of humility, and even death. Because He became like us, He connects with us. Like Jesus, we are called to participate in the transformation of the world by living as sons and daughters of God. We need to learn to tell our stories—of love and loss, and faith and hope—so that others will know that Jesus offers to them the same hope He has given to us.

> *"How, then, can they call on the One they have not believed in? And how can they believe in the One of whom they have not heard? And how can they hear without someone preaching to them?* **Romans 10:14**

Larry writes, "Everyone has a personal story they can use to connect with their team. I encouraged them (leadership at Waste Management) to let their actions show they knew how to put empathy into action, and if they modeled that behavior, the rest of the team would follow." (*Management Waste*, p. 82)

1. Do you have a personal story that helps others connect with you and demonstrates how Jesus has transformed you?

_____

_____

_____

2. What is an empathetic action you can take this week?

_____

_____

_____

3. Jesus said others will know we are Christians by the love and caring we show others (**John 13:35**). If a survey was taken in your organization about you, would the respondents answer that they know you are a Christian because of the love, caring, and empathy you show to others? What would the same survey of your friends and family say about you?

_____

---

---

4. How do you think your work team or family will remember you? It doesn't matter what you were yesterday. What changes do you want to make beginning today to change or improve that?

---

---

---

## *Pray*

Please close your session in prayer in whatever manner your group chooses. You can select one person to open and close the prayer, with others speaking up with their own prayers in between, or break into pairs to pray in groups of two, or anything else you may decide. Remember, it doesn't matter what you have been in the past, what are you going to ask the Holy Spirit to help you change beginning today? Following are suggestions to include in your prayer from this Chapter:

- God, show us how to be more compassionate, empathetic followers of Christ, reflecting to others the love You have shown to us.

- Lord, give me more opportunities to get to know people on a personal level. Teach me to become good at asking questions that lead to understanding others, and an opportunity to share with them what You have done for me.

- Lord, help me see the vision You have for my life, for my family, or for my organization, and fill me with the willingness to change what needs to change for that vision to become a reality.

- God, help me learn to listen to Your voice and hear what You are asking me. May that deeper relationship with You lead me to Your grace and align my life with Your will.

- We pray this in Jesus' Name. Amen!

## Additional Notes

# The Loneliest Job in the World

## Accountability

### *Making Connections*

In Chapter 6, Larry discusses the fourth characteristic of Servant Leadership: *Accountability*. Larry asserts that ascending to a level of leadership can become one of the loneliest positions you will ever have. Leaders feel both accountable to and responsible for the people they are leading—and often find themselves with no one to talk to about the stresses and challenges they face. To avoid isolation, every leader needs a coach/mentor in their career AND a spiritual coach/leader who can lead them as a disciple of Jesus.

### *Reflection Questions:*

It is Management Waste for Christians, who have God living inside of them, not to access Him and turn control over to Him.

- What is God nudging you to release to Him?

_____

_____

_____

- Is lack of accountability to God's loving guidance causing problems at work or home?

  _____

  _____

  _____

- What are areas in your life that you are hanging on to the controls with self-reliance rather than trusting Him?

  _____

  _____

  _____

Jesus is the ultimate mentor! If you will just turn to Him and seek His will!

## Management Waste

It is management waste to be placed into a position of authority and then not be willing to submit to God's authority and follow God's design of Servant Leadership in our position of authority. Will you consider sharing with your group an area where you lack accountability to God's loving guidance and continue to cling to self-reliance that could be causing problems at work or at home?

_____

_____

_____

## Scripture Study

### The Life of Joseph: Genesis 37-50

**Genesis 37-50** is the longest cycle of stories in Genesis. The story takes a bit of time to read, but it will be well worth your time. Jacob was the grandson of Abraham and son of Isaac. God later gave Jacob the name Israel. Jacob's 12 sons were shepherds (and they are the beginning of the 12 tribes of Israel). Joseph was his father's favorite son and as a result, his brothers "hated" Joseph (**Genesis 37:4**). In a vicious plot that stops just short of murder, the brothers sell Joseph to Egyptian traders, who in turn sell Joseph as a slave to Potiphar, who was a captain of Pharaoh's guard. While the brothers believe they will never see Joseph again (and make up a story of Joseph's death for their father), Joseph is very much alive. In many ways, his story has just begun at this point. What follows is a story of ups and downs—down into slavery, up to Potiphar's right-hand man in charge of Potiphar's possessions, down to a prison dungeon when he was wrongfully accused of attempted rape of Potiphar's wife, and then back up to Pharaoh's court and his ultimate vindication as Joseph essentially became prime minister of Egypt—resulting in Pharaoh telling Joseph that no one is as wise as Joseph (**Genesis 41:39**).

You never hear Joseph complain about his circumstances, and it is clear that God was working His plan through Joseph. A severe famine came throughout the land, and Joseph, as prime minister, had saved up grain to have for the famine. In an unexpected twist to the story, Joseph's brothers travel to Egypt to get grain for the family during the famine, since they heard there was grain there. They certainly didn't expect to find Joseph there as the prime minister!

Joseph's brothers don't recognize him immediately, and as Joseph reveals his true identity to his brothers, Joseph tells them: "So then, it was not you who sent me here, but God. He made me father to Pharaoh, lord of his entire household and ruler of all Egypt" (**Genesis 45:8**). In **Genesis 50:20**, Joseph tells his brothers: "You intended to harm me, but God intended it for good to accomplish what is now being done, the saving of many lives." In the hindsight view, Joseph sees that God has made good come out of his suffering, preserving the life of his family and many other 'families of the earth.' He affirms that God can be trusted to guide events toward the fulfillment of God's promises, often working in hidden and unexpected ways, even at times turning evil into good.

There are many lessons from Joseph's lonely life as a developing leader that followers of Christ would do well to obey. Scan the entire narrative, looking for an example or two that resonate with you. Be prepared to share them with your group and choose one to focus on and live with by faith this week. Here are some ideas:

1. Reuben convinces his brothers not to murder 17-year-old Joseph. How might I protect or defend a brother or sister in danger or who may be going through a difficult time? (**Genesis 37:18-24**).

---

---

---

2. Joseph remains sexually pure in the face of great temptation from Potiphar's wife. How can I safeguard my mind and body from sexual harm to myself and others? (**Genesis 39**).

---

---

---

3. Joseph was misunderstood and endured false accusations, yet he never complained. How can I turn to God for refuge and peace when I am misunderstood or going through a difficult time, and take comfort by looking for the *what* (what is God

trying to teach me here) rather than the *why* (why is God allowing this to happen to me)? (**Genesis 39**).

---

---

---

4. Joseph made the most of his opportunities while in prison. What are some ways I can distinguish myself as an ambassador for Christ, and allow God to use my gifts, even in undesirable or difficult situations? (**Genesis 39:19-41:45**).

---

---

---

5. Joseph trusted God with a greater plan for his life and the life of his family. Can I trust that God has a big picture in mind for me? (**Genesis 45:1-20**).

---

---

---

## *Servant Leadership*

Larry shares about his relationship with his late mentor, Jim Woods, the former Chairman and CEO of Baker Hughes. Jim created "a penalty-free environment" for Larry to ask questions and allow Jim to ask him questions to help guide his thinking.

1. Use Larry's definition of a mentor (broken down in Question 2 below) to describe a current struggle in your life.

---

---

---

2. Does someone come to mind who could serve as your mentor?
   - Someone to help guide you and coach you . . . give you insight from a different perspective . . . ask the right questions without giving you the answer to help you think through the challenge . . . to share your struggles and give you support and encouragement . . . to help you deliver on your accountability to others . . .

---

---

---

3. Who is somebody you could pour into and serve as a mentor? Who could you help guide in their current career situation or other challenging circumstance?

---

---

---

4. Who could you disciple to help them grow and mature in their faith so that they can become disciple-makers?

---

---

---

5. Think of some names and then pray that God will put the right person in your life.

---

---

---

## *Pray*

Use the "Talking to God" section of Chapter 6 as a guide to prayer in your group time. Members of the group may have highlighted other prayer prompts they will want to share.

- From **James 1:5**: Lord, You tell us to ask You for wisdom when we lack it and You will give us wisdom generously, without finding fault.

- From **Luke 5:16**: "Jesus often withdrew to lonely places and prayed." Lord, help us carve out time to pray throughout the day each day.

- In **Luke: 6:12-13**: "Jesus went out to a mountainside to pray, and spent the night praying to God. When morning came, He called His disciples to Him and chose twelve of them, whom He also designated apostles." Lord, help us remember to come to You in prayer to find discernment when facing big decisions as leaders.

- Jesus poured out His heart to God the Father, but then prayed for God's will to be done (**Matthew 26:39**). Lord, thank You for listening to our wants and desires in our prayers. Please give us the ability to listen for Your will and follow it.

- **I Thessalonians 5:17** says to "pray without ceasing." Lord, may prayer become like breath for us—a constant lifeline—so that we pray at all times, in all places, in every circumstance.

- From **James 5:16**: "Therefore confess your sins to each other and pray for each other so that you may be healed. The prayer of a righteous person is powerful and effective." Lord, just as we pray for each other in our group, may we also be given opportunities to pray with our spouse, family members, friends, co-workers, and neighbors.

- Father, put someone in my life that could serve as a business and spiritual mentor to me. And also put someone in my life that I can pour into through mentorship and discipleship to help them grow in their faith, become disciple-makers, as well as encourage and support them as they face their own struggles that you have already taught me and brought me through.
- We pray in Jesus' Name. Amen!

## *Additional Notes*

## CHAPTER 7

# "Dumbster"

## Notice

### *Making Connections*

In Chapter 7, Larry discusses the fifth characteristic of Servant Leadership: *Notice*. The first step a Servant Leader must take to improve in this area is to take the focus off himself or herself. Once the focus has shifted from self to others, the Servant Leader can begin to truly get to know people on a personal level by making an intentional effort to speak with the goal of empathetic two-way communication and learn more about the other person's point of view, experiences, and feelings.

### *Reflection Questions:*

The definition of dumb is "being unable or unwilling to speak." Larry advocates for Servant Leaders to put aside their unwillingness to move relationships to a deeper level.

- How do you rate your willingness to communicate deeper with co-workers, family, and friends?

- Think about how God wants to utilize you as His instrument in each of those relationships as His ambassador. What could you do to improve?

_____

_____

_____

## Management Waste

As you prepare to meet with your group, think about workplace barriers, attitudes, or habits you have formed that restrain you from noticing the people God has placed in your life and the relationships God has given you. Think about how God wants to utilize you as His instrument in each of those relationships as His ambassador. Consider sharing with the group one of your struggles in this area.

## Scripture Study

**Philippians 2:1-11**

> *Therefore if you have any encouragement from being united with Christ, if any comfort from His love, if any common sharing in the Spirit, if any tenderness and compassion, [2] then make my joy complete by being like-minded, having the same love, being one in spirit and of one mind. [3] Do nothing out of selfish ambition or vain conceit. Rather, in humility value others above yourselves, [4] not looking to your own interests but each of you to the interests of the others.*
>
> *[5] In your relationships with one another, have the same mindset as Christ Jesus: [6] Who, being in very nature God, did not consider equality with God something to be used to His own advantage;[7] rather, He*

*made Himself nothing by taking the very nature of a servant, being made in human likeness. [8]And being found in appearance as a man, He humbled Himself by becoming obedient to death—even death on a cross!*

*[9]Therefore God exalted Him to the highest place and gave Him the name that is above every name,[10] that at the name of Jesus every knee should bow, in Heaven and on earth and under the earth,[11] and every tongue acknowledge that Jesus Christ is Lord, to the glory of God the Father.*

**2 Corinthians 5:20**

*We are therefore Christ's ambassadors, as though God were making His appeal through us. We implore you on Christ's behalf: Be reconciled to God.*

**John 13:35**

*By this everyone will know that you are My disciples, if you love one another.*

1. Paul wrote to the church he had established at Philippi while he was imprisoned. His major concern was to bring them together, so that their church community would not be threatened by internal disharmony. (See **Philippians 2:1-30**). To make his appeal for unity, he raises up Christ as the first example of self-emptying for the sake of others.

2. From verses 1 and 2, what qualities does Paul mention that a group of believers can enjoy when they live as though "being one in spirit and of one mind"? What would it mean to you to experience love, compassion and tenderness in a Christian community and in all your relationships with family, friends, and colleagues?

3. In verses 3 and 4, what actions and attitudes does Paul recommend that we either avoid or adopt as we attempt to honor others? Can you share an example of how you have been affected by selfish ambition or vain conceit in yourself or others? How about humility and empathy towards others or toward you?

4. The mindset of self-sacrifice that all Christians are called to adopt comes from Jesus. What phrases from this earliest of Christian hymns quoted in **Philippians 2:5-11**, highlight Christ's sacrifice? Which of these phrases best helps you grasp the selflessness of Jesus?

5. What does it mean to you that Jesus came in human form?

6. Read verses 9-11. God exalted Jesus, resurrecting Him after His death on the cross. What does it mean to you that Jesus is Lord, both on a personal basis and also as Lord of Heaven and earth?

## *Servant Leadership*

Larry shares several strategies he uses to make him a better "noticer" of people. Some are listed below. As a group, use these as a starting point for creating your own strategies for improving your ability to notice the other people who God has placed in your life—family, friends, and colleagues.

1. Writing down the names of employees he met that were ready for a bigger role and following up with their supervisor to develop a plan to help that employee progress upward in their career.

2. Remembering the command of Jesus to "go and make disciples" in **Matthew 28:19-20** helped Larry notice the people God placed in his path as he was going about his daily work—looking for opportunities to share his faith, and knowing Jesus was with him.

3. Noticing when colleagues were down or having a bad day, and asking if he could pray with them.

4. Developing his own self-awareness, by paying attention to how others receive him and react to him, and being willing to make needed adjustments or to draw others into the discussion.

5. Paying attention to his stress behaviors and learning to switch gears when under stress.

6. Asking someone on his team to serve as his "trusted, courageous, unvarnished truth-teller."

7. Seeking wise counsel from others to gain insight from other points of view.

8. Letting others notice you by making yourself vulnerable and transparent to others to build trust with them.

9. Taking a cue from Shane Battier, who played with the team's success as his goal rather than his own statistics.

10. Expecting that mistakes will be made when you empower others. Being willing to take the blame when mistakes are made, and giving the credit to others for the successes.

## *Lifeline Exercise*

- This week, take time to do the Lifeline Exercise. To prepare, reread *Management Waste*, pages 121-123. Also look at the template below.

- Draw a timeline of your life, starting with your childhood, moving to the present.

- Mark the major ups and downs of your life and career, and connect the dots with a line. Take your time, using the process as a time of reflection and prayer.

- Once your lifeline is complete, go back and mark with a cross symbolizing Christ, a dove symbolizing the Holy Spirit, or a heart symbolizing God the Father at the places where you now see that God was with you in the ups and downs of life.

- What was God trying to teach you, what did you learn from those experiences, and how have they shaped who you are today?

- Use your Lifeline as a way of telling your story to others with whom you wish to share at a deeper level—and a way to get to know others better by hearing their stories. You can even try this with your spouse.

Your group may choose to share the lifelines during this session—or at a different session as time allows. As you share your life and listen to the stories of others, NOTICE how your compassion and closeness as a group grows. The more vulnerable and transparent people are in their personal stories, the closer you will become in your relationship with them. Letting down your guard is not easy, but it is very powerful.

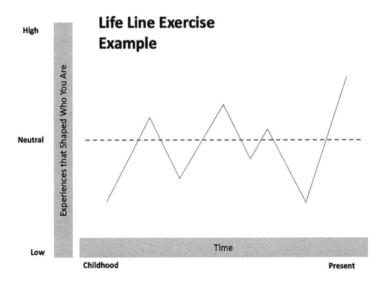

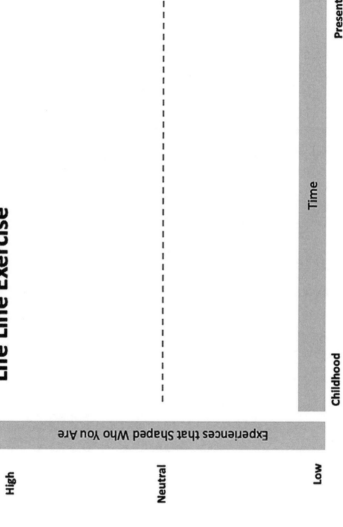

## *Pray*

Please close your session in prayer in whatever manner your group chooses. If you are doing the Lifeline Exercise, you could pray as a group for each person who shares their story. Following are suggestions to include in your prayer from this Chapter:

- Lord, thank you for creating each one of Your children with a story worthy of noticing. Give me ears to hear and eyes to see the people around me and the desire to hear their story.

- Jesus, You command Your followers to make disciples as we are going about our daily lives. Make me a disciple who makes disciple-makers. Put people in my life that You want me to serve as Your instrument to draw them into a closer relationship with You. Make me more aware of when You want me to do that. I am willing to be made willing to serve You in this way.

- Forgive me, Lord, for failing to see both the gifts and needs of the people around me. Thank You for forgiving me and filling me with Your Spirit, so that I will have more compassion.

- Lord, sometimes the person I notice the least is myself. Help me trust You more rather than relying on myself, so that I can grow in self-awareness.

- Thank You, Jesus, for coming to earth in human form — fully man and fully God. May I live in a way that proclaims You as Lord and gives You glory rather than seeking to glorify myself.

- We pray this in Jesus' Name. Amen!

## *Additional Notes*

# Recycling: One Man's Trash Is Another Man's Treasure

## Joy and Contentment Are Infectious

### *Making Connections*

There is a power that comes from being content with what God has already given you. When you begin to rely on God, and trust that God is in control and has given you everything you have, Larry says in Chapter 8, then you can experience true joy and contentment. Larry found peace and contentment through accepting God's plan for his daughter—one that was different from what Larry originally had in mind.

### *Reflection Questions*

• Rather than allowing God to fill us with contentment, most people at some point will pursue happiness apart from God. What are some ways you are currently doing this?

_____

_____

_____

• As you study this Chapter, be aware of and reflect on your sources of both contentment and discontentment.

## Management Waste

It is management waste to pour our lives into work, position, status, or material possessions, and our lives can spiral downward if the things we think will bring contentment like drugs, alcohol, pornography, excessive possessions become addictions that control us. Share as you feel led (and are comfortable) with your group about a struggle with contentment.

## Scripture Study

**A Study of Paul**

In Chapter 8, Larry presents an overview of the life of the Apostle Paul. Reread *Management Waste*, pages 132-142 and skim **Acts 9-28** as a reminder of his amazing life. Paul, who started out as a Jewish terrorist pursuing the killing of Christians because of their beliefs, was transformed after Jesus appeared to him, and he ended up writing about half of the New Testament! The introduction notes in your Bible for Acts and any of the Pauline letters are also helpful starting points. Let's look at some of Paul's key writings on the subject of contentment.

1. Read **1 Timothy 6:6-12, 17-19.**

   • What warnings does Paul point out for those who love money? (Note that verse 10 says "the love of money" (not money itself) is the root of all sorts of evil. This verse is often misquoted.)

   • What blessings are in store for those who pursue righteousness?

_____

_____

2. Read **Philippians 4:11-13.**

- Paul *learned* to be content. How is God teaching you to be content in both scarcity and plenty?

_____

_____

_____

3. Read **1 Thessalonians 5:16-18.**

- How do you think thankfulness relates to contentment?

_____

_____

_____

4. Read **Galatians 5:16-26** and **Ephesians 5:15-21.**

- More than simply drawing a contrast between right and wrong behaviors, Paul is teaching what it means to live as a Spirit-filled Christian in these passages. How are the fruits of the Spirit evidenced and even increasing in your life as you "live by the Spirit"?

_____

_____

_____

5. Read **Romans 8:31-39.**

- Paul speaks to contentment that comes from hope in Christ even in tough times. How does this passage encourage you?

_____

_____

_____

## *Servant Leadership*

1. Larry shares his own struggles in the journey to finding contentment. "I think the secret to contentment is understanding God is sovereign and in control. . . that means God is in control when good things happen in our lives, and God is in control when times are tough for us." What is a circumstance in your life that God has used to teach you contentment and to trust Him?

_____

_____

_____

2. One of the traps Larry fell into on his journey toward lasting contentment was thinking about the "what-ifs" of Linley's life. What are your "what-ifs"? Can you offer your "what-ifs" to God and find true contentment as a replacement by trusting that God is in control?

_____

_____

_____

3. The secret to contentment is our relationship with Jesus Christ. Our nature is to sin, complain, and want more than God has given us. With Christ in our lives, we can be restored more closely to God, who created human beings in His image (**Genesis 1:26-27**). How is Christ, living in you, transforming you in the area of contentment?

_____

---

## *Pray*

Please close your session in prayer in whatever manner your group chooses. Following are suggestions to include in your prayer from this Chapter:

- Thank You, God, for creating me in Your image. I give my life to You, with its sin and brokenness, trusting Christ for forgiveness. Thank You for changing me from the inside out with the help of the Holy Spirit.

- Lord, help me to turn control over to You, and rely on You, and trust in Your plan, rather than continuing to rely on myself.

- Lord, I confess my tendency to look for joy and contentment in the world. Help me learn to be content as Paul did—in all kinds of circumstances, knowing that You are in control, You love me, and will never leave me.

- When I am faced with difficult circumstances or inconveniences, help me learn to ask *What are You trying to teach me here?* rather than *"Why are You allowing this to happen to me—this is not fair!"*

- Lord, I give You thanks for . . . Help me to be content with what You have given to me, and don't allow me to be tempted to focus on the material things that I don't have.

- Lord, all that I have is Yours. Show me how to be a good steward of all that You have given to me.

- Lord, I am struggling with a powerful enemy that seeks to rob me of joy and contentment in Christ. I need Your help.

- We pray in Jesus' Name. Amen!

## *Additional Notes*

## CHAPTER 9

# Taking Out the Trash
## What Do You Need to Turn Over to God?

### *Making Connections*

At this point in the study, Larry wisely counsels the reader to set aside time to think about your leadership style, any relationships that are not where they should be, and your current relationship with God. This process calls for self-reflection and honesty, which can be difficult. When you are ready, it's time to take out the trash.

### *Reflection Questions*

- The probing question is: **What are you hanging on to that is taking up space in your brain or your life and preventing you from trusting God with everything and turning control over to Him?**

<br>

---

---

---

### *Management Waste*

Management waste happens when we fail to honestly assess where we are, so that we can truly turn over the management of our lives to God without reservation. Otherwise, we are at risk of wasting the life, opportunities, and relationships that God has given us. Are you willing to spend the necessary time and reflection to turn over all of your life to God?

---

---

---

## Scripture Study

Read the verses below and talk about the issues they address with your group members. There may be other areas of life that bubbled up for members of the group. Search the Scriptures together for Biblical counsel.

1. *Money Matters*: **Matthew 6:24; 2 Corinthians 9:71; 1 Timothy 6:7-10; Hebrews 13:5; Peter 4:10.**

2. *Wisdom*: **Proverbs 1:7; 2:1-6; 11:2; 13:10; 19:20; James 1:5.**

3. *Worry*: **Isaiah 41:10; Matthew 6:25-34; Romans 8:38-39; Philippians 4:6-7; Hebrews 13:5-6.**

4. *Fear*: **Joshua 1:9; Psalm 23; 27:1; 56:3-4; 118:6; Isaiah 35:4; John 14:27.**

5. *Forgiveness*: **Psalm 51; Matthew 18:21-35; Romans 12:17-21; 1 John 1:9-10.**

## Servant Leadership

As you face the issues that stand between you and a clean transparent relationship with God and other people, at each step of the way, you can ask the Lord what He wants you to know about any situation. Approaching God in prayer, you will find answers to questions like the ones listed below and on page 147 of *Management Waste*:

1. Lord, what more do You want me to know about? (describe situation)

<br><br><br>

2. What are You doing in this situation, Lord?

<br><br><br>

3. What are You trying to teach me in this situation?

<br><br><br>

4. What do I need to let go of and put my trust in You and Your plan?

<br><br><br>

5. Is there unforgiveness in my heart? Who do I need to forgive? God has forgiven me, so I need the Holy Spirit's help to find a way to forgive them. (**Matthew 18:21-35**).

<br><br><br>

6. If I were to obey Your Word and Your will, what needs to change in my life? Help make me willing to make that change. *"For it is God who works in you to will and to act in order to fulfill His good purpose."* (**Philippians 2:13**).

_____

_____

_____

7. After completing this exercise, throw away the notes you made! Thank God for all He has already given you. Be specific. Ask God to take what you wrote on the paper and trust Him to give you everything you need for it to be removed.

_____

_____

_____

8. There will be other times in your life when going through this process again will be helpful. God is faithful for our whole life journey. *"Being confident of this, that He who began a good work in you will carry it on to completion until the day of Christ Jesus."* (**Philippians 1:6**).

_____

_____

_____

## Pray

Everyone needs the support of Christian friends who are committed to praying for them. Your group can take time in this session to intercede for one another. The needs can be named or kept private. God knows what each person needs. Please close your session in prayer in whatever manner your group chooses. Following are suggestions to include in your prayer from this Chapter:

- Jesus, we trust You with all the trash in our life. Make us clean from the inside out.

- Forgive our sins (be specific if you can) and replace our weaknesses with Your strength, so that we might experience the joy of the Lord.

- Put on our hearts who we need to forgive.

- Give us the will and the way to do what You want us to do and bring glory to You and not ourselves.

- We pray in Jesus' Name. Amen!

## *Additional Notes*

## CHAPTER 10

# Exit Strategy
## When You Leave Your Job

### *Making Connections*

In Chapter 10, Larry shares his professional journey that has included career changes about every 10 years. Because he has learned to create strong teams and groom his successor, he has been able to leave to pursue his next opportunity, knowing that the company is in good hands, and allowing others to move up into new roles of increasing responsibility. Taking the initiative to pour into your team, with Jesus as your Master Teacher, will help you know when the time is right to make an exit.

### *Reflection Questions:*

- How have your experiences with team building—either as a leader or as a team member—revealed your strengths, weaknesses, and needs?

- What skills in people and roles/responsibilities do you need to surround yourself with for optimal effectiveness and success?

_____

_____

• What lessons have you learned from some of your best and worst bosses?

_____

_____

_____

• Is there someone you could be mentoring/coaching? (From Chapter 6)

_____

_____

_____

• Who could serve as your coach/mentor to help you think through the issues you are faced with in this Chapter? (From Chapter 6)

_____

_____

_____

## Management Waste

If you are contemplating leaving your current job, what are you doing now to prepare yourself, your team, and your successor? If you are new to a team, how can you contribute well? Who can you call upon to help bring you up to speed? Where do you sense any complacency or apprehension on your part?

_____

_____

_____

## *Scripture Study*

Review the Bible passages in *Management Waste* Chapter 10 that show how Jesus built His team of disciples. Discuss with your group how those strategies can be applied in your work or family team.

1. **Luke 6:12-13:** *One of those days Jesus went out to a mountainside to pray, and spent the night praying to God. [13] When morning came, He called His disciples to Him and chose twelve of them, whom He also designated apostles.*

2. **John 15:15:** *I no longer call you servants, because a servant does not know his master's business. Instead, I have called you friends, for everything that I learned from My Father I have made known to you.*

3. **Matthew 13:10-12:** *The disciples came to Him and asked, "Why do You speak to the people in parables?" [11] He replied, "Because the knowledge of the secrets of the kingdom of Heaven has been given to you, but not to them. [12] Whoever has will be given more, and they will have an abundance. Whoever does not have, even what they have will be taken from them."*

4. **Mark 3:13-19:** *Jesus went up on a mountainside and called to Him those He wanted, and they came to Him. [14] He appointed twelve that they might be with Him and that He might send them out to preach [15] and to have authority to drive out demons. [16] These are the twelve He appointed: Simon (to whom He gave the name Peter), [17] James son of Zebedee and his brother John (to them He gave the name Boanerges, which means "sons of thunder"), [18] Andrew, Philip, Bartholomew, Matthew, Thomas, James son of Alphaeus, Thaddaeus, Simon the Zealot [19] and Judas Iscariot, who betrayed Him.*

5. **Luke 22:27-30:** *For who is greater, the one who is at the table or the one who serves? Is it not the one who is at the table? But*

*I am among you as One who serves. ²⁸ You are those who have stood by Me in My trials. ²⁹ And I confer on you a kingdom, just as my Father conferred one on Me, ³⁰ so that you may eat and drink at My table in My kingdom and sit on thrones, judging the twelve tribes of Israel.*

6. **John 13:13-17:** *You call me 'Teacher' and 'Lord,' and rightly so, for that is what I am. ¹⁴ Now that I, your Lord and Teacher, have washed your feet, you also should wash one another's feet. ¹⁵ I have set you an example that you should do as I have done for you. ¹⁶ Very truly I tell you, no servant is greater than his master, nor is a messenger greater than the one who sent him. ¹⁷ Now that you know these things, you will be blessed if you do them.*

7. **Matthew 20:25-28:** *Jesus called them together and said, "You know that the rulers of the Gentiles lord it over them, and their high officials exercise authority over them. ²⁶ Not so with you. Instead, whoever wants to become great among you must be your servant, ²⁷ and whoever wants to be first must be your slave— ²⁸ just as the Son of Man did not come to be served, but to serve, and to give His life as a ransom for many.*

## *Servant Leadership*

"When it is time to move on, the best thing you can leave with is the respect of all your colleagues," says Larry. Reviewing and continuing to practice the **CLEAN** principles will strengthen you as the leader as well as the team that you lead. As you read the list below, make notes for each action item.

1. What is your next step in each of these practices?

- *Committed* to each person on your team to help them progress in their career, grow in their faith, and groom your successor.

- *Listening* to them by giving them a voice and asking them insightful questions to gain understanding.

- *Empathy* to show you care, place their interests ahead of your own, and build trust.

- *Accountable* as the leader to the team—demonstrating through your actions how to contribute to the team's success, coaching and mentoring others to be the best they can be.

- *Noticing* the people on your team by showing appreciation for their contributions, giving credit to others, and becoming more self-aware of how you come across to others.

_____

_____

_____

2. Remember, it doesn't matter what you have been in the past. How are you going to change and be different beginning right now? Share with your group one small step you want to focus on this week to help you improve as a Servant Leader.

_____

_____

_____

3. And if you are currently working under a harsh and demanding boss, listen to this podcast from Larry for encouragement: https://anchor.fm/the-larry-odonnell-podcast/episodes/1-Peter-2-All-Christians-Are-Priests-vs--Catholic-Doctrine-Dealing-with-Bad-Bosses-and-Corrupt-Leaders-e1qvjfm/a-a8t0652.

_____

_____

_____

## *Pray*

Please close your session in prayer in whatever manner your group chooses. You can select one person to open and close the prayer, with others speaking up with their own prayers in between, or break into pairs to pray in groups of two, or anything else you may decide. Remember, it doesn't matter what you have been in the past, what are you going to ask the Holy Spirit to help you change beginning today? Following are suggestions to include in your prayer from this Chapter:

- Lord Jesus, I want to follow Your example as a team leader. Help me lead like You lead and place others ahead of myself.

- Lord, please guide me to the people You want me to lead. Fill me with the Holy Spirit, so that the guidance I give and the decisions I make will come from You.

- Lord, I am thankful for the people You have placed on my team. Show me ways to express my appreciation and gratitude to them, help them be successful, and grow in their careers and personal relationship with You.

- Help me to give credit to my team and give glory to You, rather than seeking glory for myself.

- Lord, help me apply the **CLEAN** principles in my life, and help me to become an effective Servant Leader that reflects You to others. Show me where I need to change.

- Holy Spirit, please guide me as I seek Your will about my current situation at work and home. Show me clearly my best next step. Close doors that You do not want me to consider, and open doors on the path You want me to follow.

- Thank You for all the relationships You have given me with my family, friends, and colleagues. Help me see where You want to utilize me as Your instrument to draw them into a closer relationship with You, and then give me the will and the way to accomplish that.

- We pray this in Jesus' Name. Amen!

## *Additional Notes*

CHAPTER 11

# The Ultimate Undercover Boss

## Concluding Remarks

### *Making Connections*

In your final group session using this Study Guide, come prepared to share your faith story with the group. By now, you
have shared repeatedly from the heart with one another, and
there may be aspects of your life as a disciple of Christ—the
Ultimate Undercover Boss—that are already well known in the
group.

### *Reflection Questions*

- Why are you uncomfortable telling others about Jesus and the
  difference He has made in your present life and your eternity?

_____

_____

_____

- If you really love others, why do you not want to help them
  see how they can have their sins forgiven and eternal life in
  Heaven?

_____

_____

_____

• What is preventing your from trusting that the Holy Spirit will give you the words to say?

_____

_____

_____

## Management Waste

It is Management Waste to waste the opportunities that God provides to you to share your faith with others. Someone helped you come to understand what you needed to do to place your faith in Jesus as your Lord & Savior. God now wants to utilize you as His instrument to help others. This is a chance to practice sharing your faith, so that you will be ready to witness to others for Christ when God gives you opportunity. Below are some thoughts and ideas to help you get started.

## Scripture Study

Here are some key Bible verses about sharing your faith with others:

1. **Matthew 28:19-20:** *Therefore go and make disciples of all nations, baptizing them in the name of the Father and of the Son and of the Holy Spirit, ²⁰ and teaching them to obey everything I have commanded you. And surely I am with you always, to the very end of the age.* (Jesus' last words to us as Christians was to tell us that His plan is for each of us to go and tell others the Good News of the Gospel, and He will be with us to help us.)

2. **Ephesians 4:11-12 (NASB, emphasis and bracketed language supplied):** *And He gave some as apostles, some as prophets, some as evangelists, some as pastors and teachers, [12] for the equipping of the saints [all Christians] for the work of ministry, for the building up of the body of Christ.* (The Bible tells us it is the Pastor's job to equip all of us as Christians to build up the body of Christ. That is our job, not the Pastor's job).

3. **Romans 10:13-15:** *Everyone who calls on the name of the Lord will be saved. [14] How, then, can they call on the One they have not believed in? And how can they believe in the One of whom they have not heard? And how can they hear without someone preaching to them? [15] ... As it is written: "How beautiful are the feet of those who bring good news!"* (The Bible tells us that God wants to utilize us as His instruments to tell others the Good News of Jesus Christ, not just acting in a way that they see we have the light of Christ living in us, but actually opening our mouth and telling them about Jesus).

4. **Romans 10:9-10:** *If you declare with your mouth, "Jesus is Lord," and believe in your heart that God raised Him from the dead, you will be saved. [10] For it is with your heart that you believe and are justified, and it is with your mouth that you profess your faith and are saved.* (We just have to help people learn and understand what they must do to accept the free gift of forgiveness of their sins and eternal life in Heaven by making Jesus their Lord & Savior).

## *Servant Leadership*

We are true Servant Leaders when we make Jesus our Lord, Savior and Master, and we become servants of the Most-High God, and obey His command to be willing to be His instruments to help others learn about the Gospel and what they must do to be saved.

Let me (Larry) share one last story that really got me motivated and engaged to share the Gospel with as many people as I can each week. It is actually a dream/nightmare I had years ago that really got my attention. I dreamed that I had died and I was in line to go through the gates of Heaven. I was so excited to know that I had arrived and that I was going through the gates to spend eternity in Heaven with Jesus. All the people in line with me started high-fiving each other and saying "Wow! Can you believe this!?! We are about to enter the gates of Heaven!"

And then I started hearing some people calling out to me. And I looked over and saw another line of people on the other side of a huge abyss. And I saw that they were in line to go and spend eternity in Hell separated from God. And I recognized the people in that line who were calling out to me—they were family members and friends (thankfully, I don't remember exactly who they were after I awoke so I don't know exactly who of my friends and family are headed to Hell), but they were calling out to me saying "Larry, Larry, why didn't you tell us what we needed to do to be in that line with you going to Heaven while we were still alive. We thought you loved us and cared about us. Why didn't you ever say anything to us while we were alive." Then I woke up with my heart racing! And then I immediately woke up my wife to tell her what I just experienced.

I've got to tell you, that really impacted me. I don't want to have anyone I know say that I didn't say anything to them about how to be assured of having their sins forgiven and eternal life with the Lord by placing their faith in Jesus Christ as their Lord and Savior. That is one of the reasons I wrote *Management Waste: 5 Steps to Clean Up the Mess and Lead with Purpose* and this Study Guide. It also led me to attend Dallas Theological Seminary for 3½ years after my business career to earn my degree, and now I spend most of my time in ministry helping others. And nothing has brought me greater joy than what I am doing now to help others find and/or grow in their relationship with the Lord.

So who do you know that you could say something to and allow God to utilize you as His instrument to change their eternity? Who could you pour your life into? What role does God want you to be playing in His plan? Why has He given you the relationships that you have? I encourage you to think and pray about that. We are all going to have to stand before the Lord and give an accounting of how we used the opportunities and gifts that God has given us (as Christians, not in judgment for our salvation, but for our rewards and responsibilities into eternity). How are you using yours?

And some of you may be saying to yourself, I truly want to do this, but I just don't know how. Set forth below are some of the ways Larry helps others place their faith in Jesus as their Lord & Savior. These are included, not to bring glory to me, but to help you come up with your own ideas and stories that you can use to help others.

One approach is as follows:

> I really care about you (or there must be a reason that God put us together today), and I was wondering if you know where you would go if you died tonight?" And if they answer like most people, they will probably answer: "Well, I hope Heaven." And then you ask: "Why do you think God will let you into Heaven?" And they will probably respond: "Well, I try to live my life as a good person, I try to go to church every now and then (or I used to go to church, but I haven't been in a while), etc."
>
> Well there is certainly nothing wrong with trying to live your life as a good person. But if you are like me, you probably aren't perfect. You probably fall short

and have sin in your life from time to time, right? You see every single one of us is a mess deep down. Every single one of us a sinner. It doesn't matter how much science keeps developing and finding new discoveries, nobody has found a cure for sin. It impacts us all. And because of our sin, our relationship with God is not what it should be. No matter how hard we try to be good or do good things to earn our way to Heaven or to earn blessings from God, it will never be good enough. Because God demands perfection, and none of us is capable of that. None of us.

Every religion in the world (except one) says if you just do enough good stuff, then you might be good enough to get into Heaven and earn your way into a restored relationship with God—and He will let you know when you get there. So no guarantees. And you hope that God grades on the curve and will let you into Heaven because you will be just a little better than the average. Right? Maybe that is what you are thinking. Well, if that is your plan, I have very disturbing news for you. The Bible is clear that will never work. Unfortunately, if that is your plan, you aren't going to get there, even though that is what all religions of the world offer (except one).

However, I said there was one exception that is different from all the other religions in the world, and that one exception is Christianity. Let me very briefly explain. True Christianity says that God understands that we have a sin problem separating us from Him. So, He wanted to provide a pathway for us to restore our relationship with Him. Instead of us trying to be good enough to get to Him, which we will never be able to do, or do a bunch of stuff to earn our way, like going to church, and doing a bunch of religious stuff, He came down to us. He sent His Son Jesus, who lived a perfect life on this earth for over 30 years (the only one to do so) to then die to pay our debt for our sins. Jesus was then buried and rose from the dead and was seen by over 500 people before ascending back to Heaven, to prove that He was indeed God, and that His sacrifice to pay our debt that we couldn't pay ourselves was acceptable to God the Father. In other words, the debt we owe for our sin was paid up in full by Jesus' life! If we will just believe, and accept the free gift of salvation that He is offering to each of us. There are also benefits on this side too—You get abundant life on this side, and eternal life in Heaven on the other side. The decision you make about Jesus is the most important decision you will ever make.

I know it is a crazy story, but I didn't write it or make it up. I'm just telling you about it so you can decide for yourself if you want to accept this free gift from God. But it's not yours unless you accept it. Just as if I offer you this watch on my arm as a free gift. It's not yours unless you accept and receive it.

And I have had many people tell me "Larry, you are crazy. You say that God is a loving God, and so if He is truly a loving God, He would not send anyone to Hell. All paths lead to God." And I say "Yes, God is a loving God, that is why He is offering you a free gift of the forgiveness of your sins, and a pathway to restore your relationship with Him, and the promise of eternity with Him in Heaven. It is your choice and your decision to either accept the free gift that He offers, or reject what God is offering you. And you are correct that all paths lead to God—We will all stand before Him at the end of our life here—But only those who accepted His free gift and placed our faith in His Son as our Lord and Savior and have our sins forgiven will go to Heaven for eternity with God. Those who reject God's Son will live into eternity separated from God. All are invited, but not all want to accept the invitation for some reason. Heaven and Hell will both be filled with people who lived their lives on earth as sinners (we are all sinners)—the difference is that those in Heaven had their sins forgiven by choosing Jesus as their Lord and Savior and accepting His free gift of the forgiveness of their sins and eternity in Heaven with Him. I hope I am not offending you, and I didn't write this plan. I am just sharing with you what God has told us in His Bible.

And it is not a decision you can avoid making. Doing nothing is making a decision to do nothing, and it has impacts in this life and beyond. It is that important. And I want you to know that I could not have made it through all the difficulties I have faced in my personal life and in my career, had I not made this decision early in my life. I am not telling you what you have to believe, and you are free to believe whatever you want to believe. That is between you and God. But I wanted you to at least hear this and consider this because I truly care about you, and I at least want you to think about it and consider it, because it changed my life (Be prepared to explain how your life has changed), and it changed my eternity. And maybe it can help you. Now, because of the peace I have found, when difficult times come my way, I no longer ask why? I ask what? What is God trying to teach me through this difficulty. It has been a game changer for me, and I hope you will find it a game changer for you.

It is about a personal relationship with Jesus Christ, not doing a bunch of things trying to earn your way. Would you like me to help you place your faith in Jesus Christ as your Lord and Savior? Do you have any questions I can help answer for you? Is there any reason you wouldn't want to accept that free gift that Jesus is offering right now?

And if they say yes, you can use anything along the lines of the simple prayer on page 174 of *Management Waste* and pray with them. Then offer to help them find a church or invite them to attend church with you.

If they say they are not ready right now to do that, tell them you appreciate them hearing you out. Tell them if they feel a little something on their heart, it may the Holy Spirit inviting them into a personal relationship with Jesus Christ. Tell them:

Don't say no to God's invitation, and don't put Him off. Jesus wants a personal relationship with you. You can just pray this simple prayer: "God, I don't know if you are really out there, but if you are, and if what Larry is saying is true, I am willing to be made willing. Please put the truth in my heart, and if what Larry is saying is indeed true, please make me willing to accept your free gift and help me make Jesus Christ my Lord and Savior.

And if you have any questions, or would like to discuss this further, here is my phone number. Call me anytime. I would love to help you find the answers to any of your questions, so that you can have the peace that I have found. It is a game changer. I am only telling you all this because I care about you. So think about it, talk to your friends and family about it, pray about it, but make an informed decision. Thank you for hearing me out and at least considering this for your own life.

The above can be modified in any way you want to tell your story of how Jesus has changed you. Some of the verses I sometimes work into the discussion are these:

- **John 3:16**: *For God so loved the world, that He gave His one and only Son, that whoever believes in Him will not perish, but will have eternal life.*

- **Romans 10:9**: *If you confess with your mouth, 'Jesus is Lord,' and believe in your heart that God raised Him from the dead, you will be saved.*

- **John 14:6**: *I am the way, the truth, and the life. No one comes to the Father except through Me.*

Another approach is to begin by saying: "Do you have a minute for me to tell you my story and one of the most important decisions I made in my life?" And then just tell your personal story of how you were led to Christ, how things were before, and the peace you have now, even through your trials and difficulties.

Another approach I have used a lot is to simply ask the person if there is something going on in their life that you can pray for. I can't tell you how many times the person has then broken down into tears to tell me about some tragedy they are dealing with. I am then able to tell them how my faith in Jesus helped me through my tragedy with Linley. I share the Gospel with them and invite them to pray the sinner's prayer along the lines of the prayer on page 174 of *Management Waste*.

Another approach I have used when giving talks to large groups is as follows:

> So, I know we all know this but many people give this little thought. We know that we are all going to die eventually, (unless the Lord returns before we die), right?? I also know that with a group this size, we have many different religious beliefs and denominations represented, and some that are just agnostic, or just don't want to think about death or what happens after death. I'm not here to offend anyone, but the next few minutes, I'm going to share my personal experience of avoiding catastrophic loss, and by that, I mean what happens after our life here. So please, if any of you find what I am saying in our concluding minutes offensive, please don't hesitate to leave quietly. But if you possibly can, I would ask that you at least hear me out in these concluding minutes.
>
> I am going to guess that many of you have purchased medical insurance to help you minimize your costs when you get sick, perhaps you have purchased homeowner's insurance to cover your potential exposure in the event there is a catastrophic loss of your home, and perhaps many of you may even have purchased life insurance. So I bet most of you have thought about how to avoid or minimize your risk from catastrophic losses in some way. So let me ask you this—how do you insure that when you die, you can absolutely, positively avoid the catastrophic loss of going to hell for eternity? And absolutely, positively guarantee that you go to Heaven to be with God for eternity? Call it an Eternal Life Insurance Policy. Do you have an insurance policy for that? If

there was an insurance policy for that, would you be interested? Would you want to be covered? Would you want your friends and family to have a policy like that?

What if I told you that such a policy is indeed available! And what if I told you that the cost of the policy is absolutely free!! Yes, you heard me right, it is free!! Many people won't buy life insurance because it is too expensive. But if I could sell you a $10 million life insurance policy for $100 would you buy it? Of course you would! But the policy I am telling you that is being offered to you is a policy that guarantees your eternal life in Heaven with God, and the cost is absolutely free to you! Why would anyone say no to a policy like that??? And if you don't accept this free policy, then by default you have chosen the eternal death policy, rather than the free policy I am telling you about, and the eternal death policy you pay for forever. You heard me right—you continuing paying for eternity while you are separated for eternity from God. Seems like a simple choice to me? Why wouldn't everyone want the free policy of eternal life?

Now you may be thinking that I've lost my mind, or that sounds too good to be true. Well it is crazy, but it is true! Just hear me out for just a couple of minutes more.

You see we are all sinners. Every single one of us a sinner. It doesn't matter how much science keeps developing and finding new discoveries, nobody has found a cure for sin. It impacts us all. And because of our sin, our relationship with God is not what it should be. No matter how hard we try to be good or do good things to earn our way to Heaven or to earn blessings from God, it will never be good enough. Because God demands perfection, and none of us is capable of that. None of us. Every religion in the world (except one) says if you just do enough good stuff, then you might be good enough to get into Heaven and earn your way into a restored relationship with God—and they will let you know when you get there. So no guarantees. And you hope that God grades on the curve and will let you in because you will be just a little better than the average. Well, if that is your plan, I have very disturbing news for you. The Bible is clear that will never work. And there is no insurance policy you can buy to insure against that risk if that is your plan. You have chosen the Eternal Death Policy by default.

However, I said there was one exception that is different from all the other religions in the world, and that one exception is Christianity. True Christianity says that God understands that we have a sin problem separating us from Him. So, He wanted to provide a pathway for us to restore our relationship with Him. Instead of us trying to be good enough to get to Him, which we will never be able to do, He came down to us. He sent His Son Jesus, who lived a perfect life on this earth for over 30 years (the only one to do so) to die to pay our debt for our sins. He then was buried and rose from the dead and was seen by over 500 people before ascending back to Heaven, to prove that He was indeed God, and that His sacrifice to pay our debt for us that we couldn't pay was acceptable to God the Father. In other words, the premium for the Eternal Life Insurance Policy that I am talking about was paid up in full by Jesus' life! And this policy is the only life insurance policy that I am aware of that there can only be one beneficiary, and the benefits of the policy can only go to the deceased after their death! However, there are also benefits on this side too—You get abundant life on this side, and eternal life in Heaven on the other side.

I know it is a crazy story, but I didn't write it or make it up. I'm just telling you about it so you can decide for yourself if you want to accept this free gift from God and a paid-up in full insurance policy guaranteeing your eternal life in Heaven when you die. (A copy of the Eternal Life Insurance Policy is below.) All you have to do is to pray a simple prayer along the lines of the prayer at the top of the page of the Eternal Life Insurance Policy, and truly believe it in your heart. And then you will receive the benefits that are outlined in the policy. And the fine print at the bottom of the policy (like the boilerplate you see in insurance policies) are the verses from the Bible that support everything that is written in the policy. So what is keeping you from praying that prayer today, and making Jesus Christ your Lord and Savior? Can I help you do that today?

And maybe you just aren't ready to do that today. And let me say to you, thank you for hearing me out. But if at least some of what I have said seems to be weighing on your heart, I would ask you to pray to God and simply say, "God, I don't know if You are really out there, but if You are, and if what Larry is saying is true, I am willing to be made willing. Please put the truth in my heart, and if what Larry is saying is indeed true, please make me willing to accept your free gift." Here is my phone number, and please feel free to call me anytime if I can help you find answers to your questions. I care about you, and just want to help you.

Review the Eternal Life Insurance Policy on the next page and write down some ideas of how you can use any of the above approaches to share the Gospel message with others along with your own story.

## ETERNAL LIFE INSURANCE POLICY

**BE IT KNOWN, THAT IF YOU,** the Holder of this **Eternal Life Insurance Policy,** have truly believed, confessed from your heart, and prayed to God, that:

"Lord, I know I am a sinner, and I know I am lost without You. I need Your forgiveness. I know You can take me and all my past mess ups and turn my life into something good. I believe You sent Your Son Jesus, who came and lived a perfect life on this earth, died on the cross to pay for my sins, was buried and rose on the third day. God, I need forgiveness, because I see that I am lost without You. I receive Your gracious free gift of eternal life and the forgiveness of my sins, which were bought and paid for by Jesus Christ, Your Son, in whom I have placed my faith. Thank You for Your unmerited grace and love toward me. I thank you that the Holy Spirit has come to live in me and has begun to work in my life to change my heart, and to change me so that I can make a difference in the world around me. Help me bring glory to You Father, in the way I act and the words I use at work, and with my family and friends. I pray this in the name of Jesus Christ, Your Son, our Lord and Savior. Amen!"

**THEN YOU ARE PROMISED THAT YOU HAVE RECEIVED THE FOLLOWING <u>FREE</u> GIFTS FROM GOD:**

- Your sins (past, present, and future) are forgiven;
- You have eternal life with Jesus Christ; and
- You have been given the Holy Spirit to live in and through you to begin to change you into the person that God intends you to be through a process that will continue until the first to occur of your death or the return of Jesus Christ.

**BELIEVED, CONFESSED, PRAYED, AND SIGNED THIS _____ DAY OF _____, 20__.**

_____
Printed Name:
Title: Servant of Most High God, Citizen of Heaven

**GUARANTEES FROM GOD:**

"For God so loved the world, that He gave His one and only Son, that whoever believes in Him will not perish, but will have eternal life." John 3:16

"If you confess with your mouth, 'Jesus is Lord,' and believe in your heart that God raised Him from the dead, you will be saved. For it is with your heart that you believe and are justified, and it is with your mouth that you confess and are saved." Romans 10:9-10

"For it is by grace you have been saved, through faith—and this is not from yourselves, it is the gift of God—not by works, so that no one can boast." Ephesians 2:8-9

"And you also were included in Christ when you heard the word of truth, the gospel of your salvation. Having believed, you were marked in Him with a seal, the promised Holy Spirit, who is a deposit guaranteeing our inheritance until the redemption of those who are God's possession—to the praise of His glory." Ephesians 1:13-14

"We have been made holy through the sacrifice of the body of Jesus Christ once for all." Hebrews 10:10

"To all those that received Him and believed in His name, He gave the right to become children of God." John 1:12

"Just as man is destined to die once, and after that to face judgment, so Christ was sacrificed once to take away the sins of many people; and He will appear a second time, not to bear sin, but to bring salvation to those who are waiting for Him." Hebrews 9:27-28

"If we claim to be without sin, we deceive ourselves, and the truth is not in us. If we confess our sins, He is faithful and just and will forgive us our sins and purify us from all unrighteousness. If we claim we have not sinned, we make Him out to be a liar, and His word has no place in our lives." 1 John 1:8-10

"When you were dead in your sins and in the uncircumcision of your sinful nature, God made you alive with Christ. He forgave us all our sins, having canceled the written code, with its regulations, that was against us and that stood opposed to us; He took it away, nailing it to the cross." Colossians 2:13

"And I will ask the Father, and He will give you another Counselor to be with you forever—the Spirit of truth. The world cannot accept Him, because it neither sees Him nor knows Him. But you know Him, for He lives with you and will be in you." John 14:16-17

If you have questions or would like more information, please contact Larry O'Donnell at larry@larryodonnell.com or visit my website at www.larryodonnell.com.

## *Let's Take Action!*

In this final session, pick a partner and practice by taking turns, with one of you being the Christian believer obeying Jesus' command to share the Gospel and be a witness for Him by sharing your story to the other non-believer. And then switch roles and the person who played the non-believer role playing the Christian believer role sharing the Gospel and telling their story to the person now playing the non-believer role. The more times you do this, the better you will become at it. And remember, the Holy Spirit will give you the words, and will be working on the heart of the person you are talking to. It is not your job to convert anyone (that is the job of the Holy Spirit). Your job is to simply plant the seeds. That takes tremendous pressure off of you.

## *Pray*

Please close your session in prayer in whatever manner your group chooses. You can select one person to open and close the prayer, with others speaking up with their own prayers in between, or break into pairs to pray in groups of two, or anything else you may decide. Remember, it doesn't matter what you have been in the past, what are you going to ask the Holy Spirit to help you change beginning today? Following are suggestions to include in your prayer from this Chapter:

- Lord Jesus, I want to follow Your example as a team leader. Help me lead like You lead and place others ahead of myself.

- Lord, please guide me to the people You want me to lead. Fill me with the Holy Spirit, so that the guidance I give and the decisions I make will come from You.

- Lord, I am thankful for the people You have placed on my team. Show me ways to express my appreciation and gratitude to them, help them be successful, and grow in their careers and personal relationship with You.

- Help me to give credit to my team and give glory to You, rather than seeking glory for myself.

- Lord, help me apply the **CLEAN** principles in my life, and help me to become an effective Servant Leader that reflects You to others. Show me where I need to change.

- Holy Spirit, please guide me as I seek Your will about my current situation at work and home. Show me clearly my best next step. Close doors that You do not want me to consider, and open doors on the path You want me to follow.

- Thank You for all the relationships You have given me with my family, friends, and colleagues. Help me see where You want to utilize me as Your instrument to draw them into a closer relationship with You, and then give me the will and the way to accomplish that.

- We pray this in Jesus' Name. Amen!

## *Additional Notes*

# Closing Thoughts

It is my hope and prayer that you have found *Management Waste: 5 Steps to Clean Up the Mess and Lead with Purpose* and this Study Guide helpful, and that you now have an even closer personal relationship with Jesus from working through the Scriptures, your self-reflection, the sharing within your small group, and your prayers.

So who do you know that you could say something to and allow God to utilize you as His instrument to change their eternity? Who could you pour your life into? What role does God want you to be playing in His plan? Why has He given you the relationships that you have? I encourage you to think and pray about that. We are all going to have to stand before the Lord and give an accounting of how we used the opportunities and gifts that God has given us. How are you using yours?

Let me close by leaving you with something I want you to seriously reflect on. We each get to determine what type of leader, colleague, friend, parent, or spouse we want to be and be remembered for. How do you want to be remembered? Do you want to be someone that everyone clearly sees Christ living in and through by the way you truly care and love others, and place their interests before your own? Why does God have you in the position that you are in? How could He use you if you began to live your life as a servant to others, giving up control and self-reliance, and letting God be your leader! That is true Servant Leadership!

It doesn't matter what you have been in the past. The question is what type of leader, colleague, parent, and spouse are you going to become, beginning today? What changes are you going to make in your life? You can begin to make changes today! Just give the **CLEAN** principles a try and see what the Lord can do when you allow Him to work in your life in a big and powerful way, rather than going through the rest of your life as Management Waste (wasting your time, your life, your relationships, and the opportunities that God has given to you.)

If you have any questions that remain unanswered or want to talk to me about this further, I would love to speak to you to help you in any way I can and help you find answers to your questions. You can reach out to me on my website: www.larry odonnell.com or send me an email: larry@larryodonnell.com.

And if you have enjoyed *Management Waste* and this Study Guide and are interested in some of my other resources I make available to you for free, I have a weekly Bible Study podcast and a weekly blog on Servant Leadership that you can sign up to receive on my website: www.larry odonnell.com. I also have videos of other talks I have given. There is also one podcast lesson where I will take you from Genesis to Revelation, the entire Bible Grand Narrative Story in just over an hour, called Bible Grand Narrative posted on the August 16, 2021 podcast on my website.

May God bless you as a result of your study of *Management Waste: 5 Steps to Clean Up the Mess and Lead with Purpose* and God's Word with a group of trusted friends.

Larry O'Donnell III
June 2023

# Larry O'Donnell III Short Bio

Larry O'Donnell is now a popular speaker, author, and ministry leader after his 40+ year successful business career. He is best known for appearing as CBS' first *Undercover Boss*.

Larry was born, raised, and spent most of his career in Houston, Texas. He received his Engineering Degree from The University of Texas, followed by law school. Larry started his career practicing law (business transactions, mergers & acquisitions, securities and real estate) for almost 10 years. He then wanted to focus on a business career and moved to Baker Hughes Incorporated, the 3rd largest energy services & technology company in the world for about 10 years.

In January 2000, Larry was recruited to Waste Management Inc. (one of the largest environmental, waste, recycling, and renewable energy companies in the world) as part of a new management team to help turn around the $13.5 billion company after it had failed as one of the largest corporate blow-ups in history at that time. During his tenure at Waste Management, Larry was the first Undercover Boss featured on the CBS network hit series *Undercover Boss* which initially aired after the Super Bowl in 2010 to a still record of 38.6 million viewers.

In 2010, Larry retired from Waste Management and returned to the oilfield to pursue an entrepreneurial endeavor, and was the founder of a new start-up oilfield services company called Rockwater Energy Solutions, which grew to over $1 billion in revenue and is now part of a public company. There he served as Chairman of the Board, CEO, and President. Rockwater was also recognized as a multiple-year recipient of the *Houston Chronicle*'s Top Places to Work, and Larry was awarded the Ernst & Young Entrepreneur of the Year Award.

Larry also served on various Boards of Directors during his career, including roles of Chairman of the Board, and member of the Audit and Compensation Committees. In 2017, Larry retired from his business career to help care for his special needs daughter who was facing life-threatening medical issues.

After his daughter's recovery from her life-threatening medical situation, Larry decided to go back to school, this time seminary. Following his graduation from Dallas Theological Seminary, he now works full-time sharing what he's learned from his life's challenges and career with organizations, businesses, and churches across the nation and other countries in his public speaking, training, discipleship, and leadership events.

Larry mentors, disciples, and coaches both seasoned and aspiring leaders and pastors. He also teaches and hosts a weekly Bible study podcast (*The Larry O'Donnell Podcast*—available on Spotify and most other podcast platforms), and he writes a weekly blog on leadership, discipleship, and faith. Larry's podcast, blog, and videos of some of his prior talks can be viewed and subscribed to for free on his website: www.larryodonnell.com.

Larry's first book, *Management Waste: 5 Steps to Clean Up the Mess and Lead with Purpose*, was published in 2020, and is available in print, Ebook and AudioBook at Amazon, Barnes & Noble, and www.larryodonnell.com.

Larry and his wife, Dare, have been married for 42 years. Together, they have two children: a special needs daughter, Linley, and son, Larry IV, and his wife Christina, and their son Lawrence Reeves O'Donnell.

---

| | |
|---|---|
| Email: | larry@larryodonnell.com |
| Website: | www.larryodonnell.com |
| Facebook: | www.facebook.com/Larry ODonnellIII/ |
| LinkedIn: | www.linkedin.com/in/larry -o-donnell-44902510a. |

---